Aladdin

Adapted by Sheila Lane and Marion Kemp
Illustrations by David Anstey

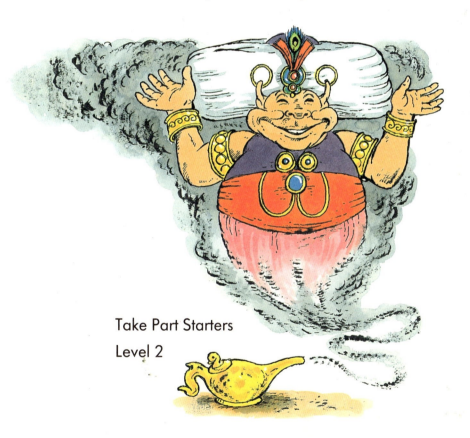

Take Part Starters
Level 2

Ward Lock Educational

Ward Lock Educational Co. Ltd.
T.R. House
Christopher Road
East Grinstead
RH19 3BT

A member of the Ling Kee Group
London · Hong Kong · New York · Singapore

This adaptation published 1989
© Sheila Lane and Marion Kemp
ISBN 0 7062 5117 2

All rights reserved. No part of this publication may be reproduced, stored in a retrieval system, or transmitted, in any form or by any means, electronic, mechanical, photocoping, recording or otherwise, without the prior permission of Ward Lock Educational Co. Ltd.

Printed in Hong Kong.

Contents

1   **Aladdin meets the Stranger**

2   **A Surprise for Aladdin**

3   **Aladdin meets the Slave of the Lamp**

4   **Aladdin makes his Fortune**

★ This sign means that you can make the sounds which go with the story.

Aladdin meets the Stranger

In this part of the story you will read about:

Aladdin,

Aladdin's mother,

and a Stranger, who is really a bad wizard looking for a boy to serve him.

Aladdin is wearing the new clothes which the Stranger has bought for him.

Aladdin Look at me in my new clothes!

Stranger Very fine, Aladdin! Very fine!

Aladdin How do I look, mother?

Mother You look very fine, Aladdin.

Aladdin A new shirt . . . a new pair of trousers . . . new shoes . . . and a new coat.

Mother You're in luck, Aladdin.

Aladdin I'm in luck at last.

Stranger Today we must find you a trade in the town, nephew.

Aladdin But I don't want a trade in the town.

Mother You see! I told you!
Aladdin is a bad boy!

Stranger What kind of work would you *like* to do, boy?

Aladdin I want to be a farmer.

Stranger Do you want to grow potatoes?

Aladdin No!

Mother I told you!
He's a bad boy!

Stranger Do you want to grow cabbages?

Aladdin No!

Mother There! I told you!

Stranger What DO you want to grow?

Aladdin . . . my fortune? Will I see my fortune?

Stranger You will see . . . a small lighted lamp. Take the lamp from the shelf. Blow it out and bring it back to me.

Aladdin But what about my fortune?

Stranger You will get your fortune when you have brought me the lamp. Here! Take this ring. It will protect you from all harm. Now . . . GO! ★

Aladdin It's so dark down here . . .
  . . . how much farther can it be?

If only I could see
the light from the lamp . . .

Ah! There it is!
He told me to take it down . . .
and . . . blow it out.
One . . . two . . . three . . . ★
It's out!
Now . . . back to the steps! ★

Aladdin   I want to grow peaches.

Mother   That's all he thinks about . . .
PEACHES!

Stranger   What do you know about growing peaches, nephew?

Aladdin   Well . . . nothing!

Mother   He knows nothing at all!
NOTHING!

Stranger   Then we must begin by teaching him something! Today I will take you to a peach farm, Aladdin. There you will see large, ripe, juicy peaches growing on the trees.

Aladdin   Oh, uncle! Thank you! And will I be able to come home and grow them myself?

Stranger   Of course! Of course!
Trust me and all will be well. ★

Aladdin How much farther is it to the peach farm, uncle? ★

Stranger Not much farther.

Aladdin My legs are getting tired. ★

Stranger Look around you at the beautiful countryside.

Aladdin I've never been here before, uncle. Where are we going? ★

Stranger To a place that I know well. Trust me and you will make your fortune!

Aladdin Very well, uncle.

Stranger Ah! This is the place.
Now . . . watch me, Aladdin.

Aladdin What are you doing that for, uncle?

Stranger Stand quite still, nephew.
Now . . . close your eyes!
Count very slowly to ten,
then open them.

Aladdin One . . . two . . . three . . .
four . . . five . . . six . . .
seven . . . eight . . . nine
. . . TEN!

Stranger Abra - ca - dab - ra . . .
Abra - ca - dee!
Open ground, open,
OPEN FOR ME! ★

Aladdin Uncle! You spoke
MAGIC words!
Look! the ground
is opening!
It's MAGIC! ★

Aladdin meets the Slave of the Lamp

In this part of the story you will read about:

Aladdin,   the Stranger who is pretending to be Aladdin's uncle,

and the Slave of the Lamp.

Aladdin and the Stranger are looking at some steps leading down to a small door under the ground.

Stranger Do you see that little door, Aladdin?

Aladdin Yes, I see it.

Stranger Now . . . I want you to go down the steps and open the door.

Aladdin I can't go down there on my own, uncle.

Stranger Oh yes, you can . . . and you MUST! The steps are too narrow for me.

Aladdin But, uncle! I can't . . .

Stranger Do you want to make your fortune, nephew?

Aladdin Yes!

Stranger Then trust me! Go down the steps and open the door.

Aladdin But what's on the other side of the door?

Stranger A little tunnel. Now Aladdin . . . go down . . . open the door . . . and crawl along the tunnel.

Aladdin But uncle! I can't . . .

Stranger Nephew! Do you want to make your fortune?

Aladdin Yes . . . yes . . . I do, but . . .

Stranger Then have no fear . . . and TRUST ME!

Aladdin But . . . how can I find my fortune in a tunnel?

Stranger Just do as I say. You must crawl along the tunnel until you come to a little shelf. There . . . on that shelf . . . you will see . . .

Aladdin Uncle! Uncle!
Look! I've got the lamp!

Stranger Give it to me, boy.

Aladdin Help me out first.

Stranger No! Give me the lamp,
THEN I'll help you out.

Aladdin Help me out FIRST, uncle . . .
PLEASE!

Stranger Do as I say! GIVE ME THE LAMP!

Aladdin NO!

Stranger You bad boy!
GIVE ME THE LAMP!

Aladdin NO! You want the lamp for yourself!

Stranger You bad boy! I'll shut
you down under the
ground until you come
to your senses!
★ THERE!

Aladdin Oh! Oh! Oh! ★
It's dark down here.
Oh! Oh! ★
What shall I do?
Well . . . this ring is no good to me now.
I'll take it off. ★
But it won't come . . .
I'll turn it round this way . . .

OH! OH! OH! ★ ★
WHO . . . WHO . . . ARE . . . YOU?

Aladdin and his mother are in the kitchen cleaning a big pile of pots and pans. ★

Aladdin Look mother! One . . . two . . . three . . . four . . . five . . . six! I've cleaned six pans.

Mother Now clean this one!

Aladdin Oh no! Not another one!

Mother Yes! Another one!

Aladdin But mother! This pan is clean.

Mother No, it's not!
Look! Clean it like this. ★

Aladdin It's not fair! I've cleaned the floor so that it looks like a new pin and now I have to clean all these pans.

Mother I'm cleaning them too.

Aladdin Mother!

Mother Yes?

Aladdin Can I have a peach to eat?

Mother No!

Aladdin Why not?

Mother We haven't got a peach.

Aladdin But I'm hungry and I WANT a peach.

Mother You get on with the pans, Aladdin.

Aladdin I've rubbed this pan so hard that I can see my face in it. Look!

Mother Here's another one. ★

Aladdin It's not fair! I want some money so that I can go out and buy a peach.

Mother We have no money.

Aladdin That's not true.

Mother Well . . . we have no money for peaches.

Aladdin But we DO have a little money and I know where you keep it. It's in the blue teapot.

Mother That money is not for peaches, Aladdin.

Aladdin Give me a little so that I can buy a peach, mother. Please! Give me a little or . . . I'll TAKE it! ★

Mother You bad boy! Get out of here! GET OUT! ★

Aladdin It's not fair!
I've cleaned
the floor . . .
I've cleaned
the pans . . .
and now she won't
give me a little
money to buy a
peach.

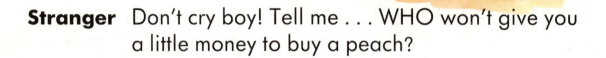

Stranger Don't cry boy! Tell me . . . WHO won't give you
a little money to buy a peach?

Aladdin My mother!

Stranger And why is that, I wonder?

Aladdin She says our money is not for peaches.

Stranger Perhaps she hasn't enough money for such
things. Do you come from a poor family?

Aladdin Yes . . . since my father died . . .

Stranger Ah! Tell me boy. What was your father's trade?

Aladdin He made coats. He was a tailor.

Stranger   A tailor, you say. Tell me boy . . . could it be that you are the son of Mustapha the tailor, by any chance?

Aladdin   Why, yes! That was my father's name.

Stranger   And could YOUR name be Aladdin?

Aladdin   Yes! But how do you know?

Stranger   I have come here to find the family of my long lost brother. I believe . . . that I am your uncle.

Aladdin   My uncle! But I didn't know I had an uncle.

Stranger   You do have an uncle, Aladdin, and he is standing here before you. Come! Shake my hand and say, 'How do you do, uncle?'

Aladdin   How do you do, uncle?

Stranger   Tell me, dear nephew . . . how is your mother?

Aladdin   She is well, uncle.

Stranger   Take me to the place where you live. I must speak to your mother at once. ★

Aladdin There's our house! It's the one with the broken gate and the paint peeling off the door.

Stranger Dear me! What a poor little place my brother lived in. Are you very poor, nephew?

Aladdin Yes, uncle! Now that my father is dead, we have no money to buy food like . . .

Stranger . . . peaches!

Aladdin How did you know about the peaches, uncle?

Stranger Your uncle knows many things, Aladdin. Here! Take this coin. Buy some peaches and then run and tell your mother that your long lost uncle is on his way to see her. ★

Aladdin Mother! Mother!

Mother What is it now?

Aladdin Look what I've got! SIX PEACHES!

Mother Where did you get them . . . you bad boy?

Aladdin I met a man who said he was my uncle. He gave me some money and I bought them in the market.

Mother UNCLE! You have no uncle!

Aladdin I have! I have! He's my long lost uncle. Look! Here he comes! ★

Stranger Greetings, dear sister! You will let me call you sister, I suppose?

Mother But . . . but . . . but . . .

Stranger No buts, sister! Come and shake my hand and tell me about my long lost brother.

Mother Your brother is . . .

Stranger Ah, yes! The butcher down the road told me that my brother is dead. Poor Mustapha! He was a tailor, I believe?

Mother Yes! He made coats.
They were good coats.

Stranger Ah, yes! Mustapha made good coats, but a poor living. Isn't that true?

Aladdin Yes, uncle! We've always been poor, but now we are *very* poor.

Stranger What about you, Aladdin? Are you going to be a tailor like your father?

Aladdin No, uncle! I don't want to be a tailor.

Mother I'll tell you about Aladdin. He's a bad boy.

Stranger How is that?

Mother He will not go out to work.

Stranger What's this, Aladdin! Do I hear that you're a bad boy who won't work?

Aladdin I don't want to be a tailor, uncle.

Mother I told you . . . Aladdin is a bad boy.

Stranger Perhaps Aladdin hasn't found work that he likes yet. Is that so, Aladdin?

Aladdin Yes, uncle! That's so!

Stranger I can see that I must be a father to you, my boy. How would you like that?

Aladdin Very much, uncle.

Stranger Very well! Tonight you must decide on a trade and tomorrow we will find work for you in the town.

A Surprise for Aladdin

In this part of the story you will read about:

Aladdin, now dressed in new clothes,

Aladdin's mother,

and a Stranger, who is pretending to be Aladdin's uncle.

Slave I am the Slave of the Lamp.
I am here . . .
to do what you ask,
that is my task.
SPEAK . . . Master!

Aladdin W . . . W . . . what do you mean?

Slave Speak, Master!
What is your wish?
Speak . . . and I obey.

Aladdin I want to get out of this place.

Slave Is that your wish, Master?

Aladdin Yes, yes! I want to get out of this terrible place and go back to my home.

Slave Your wish is my command!
★ Go from this place!
GO . . . NOW! ★

Aladdin makes his Fortune

In this part of the story you will read about:

Aladdin,

Aladdin's mother,

and the Slave of the Lamp.

Aladdin is running into the kitchen of his home, carrying the lamp. ★

Aladdin Mother! Mother! I'm home!

Mother So I see.

Aladdin And look what I've brought with me. It's a lamp.

Mother So I see!

Aladdin Mother! It's a MAGIC lamp.

Mother It's a very dirty lamp!

Aladdin Listen mother! This lamp is my fortune.

Mother It's very dirty and I don't want it in my house.

Aladdin Dirty! DIRTY! Is that all you can say! I wish I hadn't come home.

Mother You're a bad boy, Aladdin.

Aladdin But, I'm not! It's the man who said he was my uncle who is bad. He's a bad wizard!

Mother What do you mean?

Aladdin He's a bad wizard and he made me crawl along a tunnel . . . a dirty tunnel.

Mother Well . . . YOU are dirty!

Aladdin Then he shut me down in a dark hole under a big stone so that I couldn't get out.

Mother Well . . . you're here now, Aladdin! So how DID you get out?

Aladdin It was the lamp!
Mother! This lamp . . .
is . . . MAGIC!

Mother It's WHAT?

Aladdin MAGIC! That bad wizard
wanted to get it for himself.

Mother Why?

Aladdin Because it's a MAGIC lamp.
There's a slave inside.

Mother A WHAT?

Aladdin A SLAVE! And he's MY slave. He said so!
He took me out of the ground and he brought
me back home. Don't you believe me?

Mother No, I don't!

Aladdin Listen, mother! The Slave of the Lamp will do
anything I ask. You must believe me.

Mother Tell him to come out of the lamp, then.
Go on, Aladdin! Tell him to come out!

Aladdin Well . . . I don't know how to make him come out.

Mother You're a bad boy, Aladdin! You made up this story.

Aladdin I didn't!

Mother Yes, you did! And I'm not having this dirty lamp in my house.

Aladdin But . . . MOTHER!

Mother Go and get some rags.

Aladdin What for?

Mother So that we can clean the lamp. Then we can sell it.

Aladdin NO! NO! This lamp is my fortune. I'm keeping it.

Mother Then I will go and get the rags. ★

Aladdin Now . . . I must think . . . How did I get the slave out of the lamp last time? What did I do?

Mother ★ Here are the rags. I'll clean the lamp, then we can sell it.

Aladdin Mother! I've told you! This lamp is my fortune!

Mother That is what you *say*, Aladdin.

Aladdin Ah! I know! When I was under the ground I was . . . turning this ring on my finger . . . Oh! . . . OH! . . . OH! ★

Aladdin THE SLAVE!
So it *was* when I turned the ring on my finger!

Slave I am here . . .
to do what you ask,
that is my task.
SPEAK . . . Master!

Mother Go away! Go . . .

Aladdin NO, mother! Don't say that or he'll think that is your wish.

Mother It is! GO . . .

Aladdin NO! WAIT! He's a good slave. WAIT!

Mother Who . . . who . . . who are you?

Slave I am the Slave of the Lamp.

Mother Why . . . why . . . why are you here?

Slave I am here to do my Master's will.
That is my task.

Mother Who . . . who . . . who is your Master?

Slave Aladdin is my Master.

Aladdin You see, mother! This lamp is my fortune.

Mother What can this slave do, Aladdin?

Aladdin Well . . . he took me out of the ground and brought me home, so I think he can do anything.

Slave Yes. That is so, Master.
I can do whatever you ask.

Aladdin Now do you believe me, mother?

Mother I don't know . . . I don't know . . .

Slave Master! What is your wish?

Aladdin What shall I ask for, mother?

Mother Nothing!

Aladdin NOTHING! Well . . . I want SOMETHING.
I want . . . something to eat.
Watch this, mother!
SLAVE!

Slave Yes, Master?

Aladdin Bring me something to eat.

Slave What does my Master want?

Aladdin Wine . . . cakes . . . sweets . . .
fruits . . . and . . . Ah, yes!
Bring me PEACHES! Bring me
a great dish of peaches.

Slave I will do as you wish . . .
★ Come forth . . . every dish! ★

Aladdin Mother! Look at this! Wine . . . food . . . fruits of
every kind . . . grapes . . . oranges . . . dates . . .

Mother   OH, ALADDIN!

Aladdin   . . . and peaches! We shall never be poor and hungry again. SLAVE!

Slave   Yes, Master?

Aladdin   Fill up our glasses! ★

Mother What will you ask for next, Aladdin?

Aladdin I know! My coat got dirty and torn when I was crawling through the tunnel. I'll ask for a fine, new coat. SLAVE!

Slave Yes, Master?

Aladdin Bring me a new red coat . . . and bring me a fine silk dress for my mother.

Slave You shall have nothing less!
★ Come forth . . . coat and dress! ★

Mother Oh, Aladdin!
It's a fine dress.

Aladdin So don't you see, mother! We shall never be poor again. Now . . . what shall I ask for next? Would you like a fine, new house?

Mother I don't know, Aladdin.
I like THIS house.

Aladdin But it's a poor little place. Didn't that man who said he was my uncle, say so? Yes! We'll have a fine, new house.

Mother Stop! Stop, Aladdin!
You ask for too much.

Aladdin Don't worry, mother! We can trust this slave.

Mother How do you KNOW that?

Aladdin Look what he's done for us already. Don't you like this fine food and your silk dress?

Mother Well . . . yes.

Aladdin SLAVE!

Slave Yes, Master?

Aladdin I wish you to tell my mother that you are a good slave. Tell her that you will bring us no evil.

Slave ★ On this and each new day,
no evil will come your way.
It shall be as I say.

Aladdin   SLAVE! I wish for a grand, new house.

Slave   ★ In this house you will live
with the blessings I give.

Aladdin   There are you, mother! Didn't I tell you that the dirty old lamp was my fortune?

Mother   You did, Aladdin!
You did!
How happy I am!

Aladdin   And we shall live here together and be happy ever after!